T0196427

The Most of this Place

(Praise, Prayer and Power) {Acts 16:16-40}

TONI S. TROXELL

WESTBOW
PRESS®
A DIVISION OF THOMAS NELSON
& ZONDERVAN

Scripture taken from the Holy Bible, NEW INTERNATIONAL VERSION®.
Copyright © 1973, 1978, 1984 by Biblica, Inc. All rights reserved worldwide.
Used by permission. NEW INTERNATIONAL VERSION® and NIV® are
registered trademarks of Biblica, Inc. Use of either trademark for the offering
of goods or services requires the prior written consent of Biblica US, Inc.

Scripture quotations taken from the New American Standard Bible®, Copyright
© 1960, 1962, 1963, 1968, 1971, 1972, 1973, 1975, 1977, 1995 by The
Lockman Foundation. Used by permission. (www.Lockman.org)
WestBow Press books may be ordered through booksellers or by contacting:

WestBow Press
A Division of Thomas Nelson & Zondervan
1663 Liberty Drive
Bloomington, IN 47403
www.westbowpress.com
1 (866) 928-1240

Because of the dynamic nature of the Internet, any web addresses or links contained in
this book may have changed since publication and may no longer be valid. The views
expressed in this work are solely those of the author and do not necessarily reflect the
views of the publisher, and the publisher hereby disclaims any responsibility for them.

Any people depicted in stock imagery provided by Thinkstock are models,
and such images are being used for illustrative purposes only.
Certain stock imagery © Thinkstock.

ISBN: 978-1-4908-6133-3 (sc)
ISBN: 978-1-4908-6134-0 (hc)
ISBN: 978-1-4908-6132-6 (e)

Library of Congress Control Number: 2014921087

Printed in the United States of America.

WestBow Press rev. date: 09/22/2015

Contents

Preface

Nothing can substitute the Word of God. Hebrews 4:12 says, "For the word of God is alive and active. Sharper than any double-edged sword, it penetrates even to dividing soul and spirit, joints and marrow; it judges the thoughts and attitudes of the heart." God's Word is powerful, convicting, and beautiful all at the same time. For those who train by God's Word, they find comfort, guidance, and instructions for life.

With so much to find from cover to cover, where do we start? How do we apply the Bible's pages? This book has sought to take a small portion of God's Word and apply it to the here and now. *The Most of This Place* is a book for those who find themselves at a place of loss, grieving, waiting, conflict, defeat or perhaps you are ready to move to a different level with the Lord. Some of these places are more common than others. These places can be uncertain, perplexing, and confusing. We can find ourselves in some of the craziest places, and in some more than others. We may or may not have chosen these places. However, here we are. These places may last for a short time or be major places that turn our lives upside down.

God has allowed or brought us to the place where we are now. These places can be gold mines where we gain treasure if we learn to make the most of them. God has never made a mistake by putting us in these places. If we allow God to work in and through the moment, life will produce precious, Christ-centered fruit like no other.

This book will focus on Acts 16:16-40. This beautiful passage demonstrates how one can make the most of every situation. Two questions to keep in mind while reading these pages are first, "What are God's purposes or goals in the place where He currently has placed us?" and second, "What are the steps, movements, and attitudes God is trying to change to align us with His?" Prayerfully consider where you are at this moment, and ask God to help you make *The Most of this Place*.

Chapter 1

The Place of Waiting

We had the greatest weekend planned. My sister and I were meeting in South Carolina for a weekend to catch up, laugh (we love to laugh), and have fun. It had been years since we had spent real time together, and we had planned this many months in advance. She was coming from Florida and I from Virginia. I was so excited on the morning I was to leave that I could hardly wait. The phrase *hardly wait* seemed appropriate, for when I got to a certain place on I-95, the traffic was dead stopped, and there I sat for three hours. Hardly wait indeed. Oftentimes out of the blue life takes a turn, and there we sit, waiting. Up and down the highway of life there is a virtual ocean of people stepping out of their current places and looking up and down the road to access the problems they have just inherited. There they sit. And the waiting begins.

Waiting is not the number-one favorite pastime of the vast majority of people. Take a trip with me a minute and ponder this thought: Have you ever wondered what would happen if one day while hiking a trail you found yourself on the same path as a bear? Could you physically lie down and wait to see if the bear would move away? That would take a bit of courage. Our first response might be to run. Remember, the bear may outrun you, and they can climb trees.

As extreme as this may seem, waiting takes courage. Anyone can run. Anyone can hide, but only the brave can stay and wait. And let's face it; our roads are often filled with a few bears. As we venture into the book of Acts and consider the places we may find ourselves in, let's look briefly at the word *wait*.

First note some synonyms for the word wait: pause, delay, halt, rest, stay, and hold up just to name a few.[1] Which word best describes the places of waiting you find yourself at the moment? Second, consider that this waiting is not an activity others want to share. Too often the place of waiting finds us waiting in solitude. Third, waiting is one of the biggest irritants known to man. Waiting, however, is a fact of life, yet no one seems to find pleasure in it. Waiting can turn the godliest of people into a totally different people. And sometimes this is not pleasant. We want to decide when and where to wait. However, God sometimes picks us up and puts us in a place of waiting that is designed solely for

---

1   Definition of Wait in English. (n.d.). Wait: definition of wait in Oxford dictionary (British & World English). Retrieved August 10, 2014, from http://www.oxforddictionaries.com/definition.

us. This place of waiting can come from any direction and at any point of life.

As we continue to wait, questions begin to emerge, such as, "What will happen there?" "How long will I be here?" and "Why am I in this place?" These questions are normal. However, remember that God controls the door. The place where you find yourself will have a décor all its own. The colorful attitude with which we choose to decorate will set the stage for how light or dark the place will appear. We can adorn this place with bitterness, impatience, and selfishness or we can furnish this place with praise, prayer, and power. What we find and what is produced at this place of waiting depends on how we respond. God wishes to unleash His blessings and bountiful treasures (not necessarily monetary) for those who learn to wait with God and for God. These treasures can take a multitude of shapes and sizes. Yes, God can do an awesome work in the place of waiting. Yet how one waits and what one carries away is of the utmost importance.

Paul and Silas knew all too well the lessons behind waiting. As we look into one such place, we will soon realize that Paul and Silas understood that this place existed, and we will see how they responded. What they did while waiting would have lasting results. Acts 16 gives witness to a place Paul and Silas cared not to visit or remain at, and yet there they were: prison. Paul and Silas knew what could possibly happen as a result of following the Lord Jesus, but they continued to move forward. Prison is a place of waiting, holding, and uncertainty and can be a place of danger and darkness. So how did they arrive at such a place? Acts 16:19–24 shares this with us:

But when her masters saw that their hope of profit was gone, they seized Paul and Silas and dragged them into the market place before the authorities, and when they had brought them to the chief magistrates, they said, "These men are throwing our city into confusion, being Jews, and are proclaiming customs which it is not lawful for us to accept or to observe, being Romans. The crowd rose up together against them, and the chief magistrates tore their robes off them and proceeded to order them to be beaten with rods. When they had struck them with many blows, they threw them into prison, commanding the jailer to guard them securely; and he, having received such a command, threw them into the inner prison and fastened their feet in the stocks.

What a predicament! Paul and Silas were going through the city sharing Christ, and a girl who was being used to tell fortunes and obtain finances for a certain group of men began to follow them throughout the city. Not only was she following them, but she was also announcing who they were and who they served.

You might think all this free press would have been helpful, but on the contrary, Paul found it annoying. Day after day after day she continued. Still another day came, and at this point Paul had had enough and turned to the girl and commanded the spirit (in the name of Jesus) to leave the girl, and so it did. Naturally the men who used this girl were angry and wanted revenge. Their power, and the ability to praise His name (1 Corinthians 10:13, Psalm 28:7 NIV).

Paul and Silas knew this truth. They were beaten and accused, yet when the chance came to run or flee, they remained where God allowed them to be.

> But about midnight Paul and Silas were praying and singing hymns of praise to God, and the prisoners were listening to them; and suddenly there came a great earthquake, so that the foundations of the prison house were shaken; and immediately all the doors were opened and everyone's chains were unfastened. When the jailer awoke and saw the prison doors opened, he drew his sword and was about to kill himself, supposing that the prisoners had escaped. But Paul cried out with a loud voice, saying, "Do not harm yourself, for we are all here!" (Acts 16:25–28)

Remaining in the place where God has placed us comes with responsibilities and a purpose. Be content to remain in God's strength. Had Paul and Silas and the other prisoners left their place, the jailer would have died that night. Because Paul, Silas, and the others were willing to wait for God, a wonderful miracle occurred; the jailer and his family received Christ.

Staying power comes from God. Notice that Paul and Silas were waiting. At some point they decide to break out in psalms of praise. Those who were with them listened, and out of the darkness

Toni S. Troxell

came earth-shaking (literally) results. Notice it did not take a committee meeting for all of them to decide to stay put. They just did. The Scripture does not share with us how they knew to stay put, but they did. They waited for God to move. And God did. After the earthquake stopped and the gates flew open, the jailer assumed all the prisoners were gone so he decided the do what he felt was his only option—take his life. I do not hold the expertise to expand here. However, let me say if your place of waiting has brought you to a place of self-destruction, seek help now. Call your pastor, a close friend, or a help line like http://www.crisistextline. org/. Many others are here to help. Please do not delay. Remember, you are loved. Let someone help. Listen to the voice of love not the voice of despair. God is listening.

I would love to have been there for this part because I would want to see Paul, Silas, and the others just sitting there. Paul called out to the jailer, "Do not harm yourself." Our waiting may not be about us at all; it may be about another being encouraged, helped, or led to the Lord as Savior. Contentment comes when we take our eyes off ourselves and place our eyes on the one who holds our release papers—the Lord Jesus Christ. Be content to wait. The fruit will come. Praise, however you choose to do it, whether through the spoken word, music, or dance, opens the way to contentment like never before, and what a glorious power to behold when contentment comes in the midst of our waiting.

Praise

Like contentment, praise is the result when we come to a place where we trust God with the choices He has made for our lives. The other side of waiting would be called impatience. Do you remember getting a Chinese finger trap as a kid?[4] You put a finger in each end and pull. The more you pull, the tighter it becomes. The first time I did this, I thought, *How do I get out of this mess?*

When we become impatient in our waiting, praise is gone, and all we can do is cry, "God, get me out of this mess." But remember, like the Chinese finger trap, the more one struggles, the tighter and smaller the place becomes. How do you praise when the place of waiting is a job brought straight from the pit of ... well you know? Or perhaps the place is a difficult spouse. (right here I will say firmly that wherever there is abuse, get out and get help. Do not wait.) Perhaps you wait beside the bed of a dying loved one. God bless your heart. I have experienced this, and heart wrenching is an understatement.

Hold on to Jesus. Call His name. Wherever God has placed you, take with you a soul of praise. Is this easy? No. However, God through His Holy Spirit can lift your heart to this place. Now turn to Him, trust Him, and believe God (Proverbs 3:5–6). When Paul and Silas turned to praise, an amazing God thing happened. As praise began, power was released.

---

4   History of the Chinese Finger Trap. (n.d.). Chinese Finger Traps Online, Chinese Finger Puzzle Handcuffs. Retrieved October 20, 2014, from http://www.chinesefingertrap.co.uk/page_4.ht

> But about midnight Paul and Silas were praying and singing hymns of praise to God, and the prisoners were listening to them; and suddenly there came a great earthquake, so that the foundations of the prison house were shaken; and immediately all the doors were opened and everyone's chains were unfastened. (Acts 16:25–26)

When we choose to praise instead of complain, God's power is released. His power may come in the form of strength (Psalm 21:13), or it may be in the form of joy, peace, and hope "Now may the God of hope fill you with all joy and peace in believing, so that you will abound in hope by the power of the Holy Spirit" (Romans 15:13). Paul and Silas believed God and trusted Him, and this led to praise. In the middle of worship, the power of God was revealed. Are you at a place of praise in your waiting? Are you content to wait for God? Praise, contentment, and worship all lead to release. In the midst of our suffering, God wants to do amazing things in our hearts through praise. God wants to get personal with you. God wants to deliver you. Waiting … not folding, waiting … not complaining, waiting and growing.

How It Works

If you have read this far, you have not tuned me out, so that is awesome. Let me suggest a number of places to begin as you wait.

1. First, do not neglect prayer and the Word of God. As simple as this may seem, many turn their backs on these disciplines when they are in a place of waiting. Remember, while you are waiting for God to move or perhaps move you, there is an Enemy who would love to creep into your waiting place through a hole in the wall or a broken windowpane and offer to help you out that window. Satan would love to convince you that you can take the matter into your own hands and end the suffering here and now. Just follow him, and he will show you the way out.

   Remember Eve. Need I say more? A friend Satan is not, but when you have been waiting for so, so long, his lies can be quite convincing. Pay attention! Develop good, God-centered listening skills! The mail Satan delivers is meant to cause panic and confusion. The Word of God, the Bible is your breath of fresh air. Breathe it in. Do not base your praying and reading of God's Word on how rested you are or how you feel at the moment. Even if you are angry with God, go to Him and talk it over with Him. Keep reading and praying and reading and praying. God has placed you in your place of waiting for a purpose. No one else can wait for you. It must be done by you. God has an important message that only you can hear, and He is waiting to share that message with you. Stay in for the long haul. Stay focused on Christ.

2. Second, stay in church. If your waiting place is your church, don't be disobedient by forsaking fellowship (Hebrews 10:25). Keep going! Even if you need to step aside from responsibilities, do not quit God. The Enemy will be the only one winning this game. Staying power comes from God. Don't let the lies of the Enemy fuel your hurting heart. Longing to end your place of waiting can set you up for a greater disappointment. Trust God, and allow Him to show you His hand and His heart as you praise, pray, and read the Word.

3. Third, remove any "I" trouble and put your focus on another. Being centered on self (a.k.a., self-centeredness) is never of God. It is self, and it is pride. Poor, poor pitiful me is pitiful indeed. Some ideas to help self-get out of the way: a letter ministry or shuttling someone to the store or doctor's visit. Maybe you are mechanically inclined and can lend a hand with a neighbor's car or chores around the house. Maybe you are called to teach and could start a Bible study for young mothers or the homebound. Perhaps helping someone care for an aging parent or sick loved one is the place for you. Maybe it's caring for orphans and widows (a huge need). The possibilities are endless. It all depends on whether you are willing to climb out of your comfort zone called self and tend to the needs of others. The more self is dealt with, the more others will matter. Focus on others and watch praise swell in your heart and see contentment grow.

4. Fourth, as mentioned before, God has a plan for your place of waiting. Waiting can be patience. God may want you to learn a very valuable lesson that will add to your ministry. Learning to trust God reveals how much He loves us. How can I see God's love for me in this place of waiting? For years I questioned God's love for me. I grew up hardly ever feeling loved, and it followed me into adulthood and brought utter chaos to my soul. This overwhelming, heartfelt feeling was hindering my walk with my God. However, unaware and unknowing to my heart, I had been praying for this waiting place in my life. You see, God knew the only way for me to fully trust Him and know His deep love meant placing me in my place of waiting so He would have my undivided attention and begin the process of work in the shadows of my heart. Without this place, I could never have known His great love or trusted Him as I do. The begging question my Father asks is, "Do you love Me enough to wait so I can show you how much I love you?"

Are you waiting or are you waiting on someone? Has it been years? Ask God to open your heart to what He has for you. Ask Him to give you a contented heart so you may glorify His name. Resolve yourself to seek God. Don't wait for praise to come; praise Him where you are and He will honor your praise with a perfect peace only He can give (Isaiah 26:3). Let your waiting place be filled with praise and service to Him. Watch your heart change and bear fruit you never knew you had. Let's get busy in faithful praise, prayer, and study and make the most of this place.

"Restlessness and impatience change nothing except our peace and joy. Peace does not dwell in outward things, but in the heart prepared to wait trustfully and quietly on Him who has all things safely in His hands." [5]

Elisabeth Elliot

5   E. Elliot (1995). Waiting. Keep a quiet heart (p. 135). Ann Arbor, Mich.: Vine Books.

Chapter 2

The Place of Another's Soul

A play that is popular in baseball is having the hitter hit the ball in such a way that the hitter running for first base is tagged out or the ball in which he hits is a fly ball and is caught easily. In the meantime the runner on second or third base has a chance to make it home and score one for the team. This is called a sacrifice play. Sacrificing the play is common, and although the other team seems to have this knowledge, the players on the second and third bases seem to make it home. This does not, however, mean that the player who was tagged out is less important. If the hitter had not been willing to be a part of the sacrifice, the team would not have scored. Nearly every sport has a similar play.

So why is this important? "This is one of the most common plays in baseball. If you can get your team to execute sacrifice plays with regularity, then you will notice your overall run total increase considerably."[6] The idea is to bring people home, score a run, and win the game. Learning to go all the way, regardless of the cost, is the core of bringing people to the fullness of Christ and His saving grace. Salvation is witnessing to people about Christ even if the cost is painful and steep. Be willing to disciple. Take time and sacrifice for the soul purpose of another. Now this is Jesus. Being willing to stand for Christ even if it means standing alone, standing in the midst of skeptics, or standing in a lonely prison cell is what it means to sacrifice for the soul of another.

Look Who's Listening

In reading Acts 16:19–24 we see that Paul and Silas were accused of stirring up the city, humiliated in front of the whole town, beaten, and thrown into prison.

> But when her masters saw that their hope of profit was gone, *they seized Paul and Silas and **dragged them** into the market place* before the authorities, and when they had brought them to the chief magistrates, they said, "*These men are throwing our city into confusion*, being Jews, and are proclaiming customs which it is not lawful for us to accept or to

---

6   Baseball Plays: Sacrifice Play. (n.d.). Baseball Tutorials RSS. Retrieved March 3, 2014, from http://www.baseball-tutorials.com/baseball-plays-sacrifice-play/47/

observe, being Romans." *The crowd rose up together against them, and the chief magistrates tore their robes off them and proceeded to order them to be beaten with rods. When they had struck them with many blows, they threw them into prison*, commanding the jailer to guard them securely; and he, having received such a command, *threw them into the inner prison and fastened their feet in the stocks*. (Acts 16:19–24 emphasis added)

Locked up, beaten, accused, dragged around—this is a lot of physical pain, not to mention the emotional stress it places on a person. The reasons given for Paul and Silas's arrest were false. However, they proved to be effective[7].

The good news of Christ Jesus is what ultimately led Paul and Silas to prison and life-threating pain. It was in the name of Jesus that the demon was cast out of the girl. Paul and Silas were on a mission to share Jesus. It does not matter if your mission is across the world, in the workplace, or to your neighbor next door, the name of Jesus brings healing like with the girl or attacks such as with Paul and Silas. Jesus suffered so we could be with Him in heaven. Jesus died on the cross for our sins, was placed in the tomb, and rose victoriously for my sins and yours. Whether you believe this or not, this is the truth.

Paul and Silas suffered sharing this good news. They knew pain. You too may know pain associated with salvation. Whether it is physical, mental, emotional, or spiritual, pain comes to all

---

7   J. B. Polhill *Acts*. (Nashville, TN: Broadman Press, 1992), (p.352–353).

Toni S. Troxell

of us at one point or another. However, pain from sharing this precious good news is the greatest of all pain. Glorious is the feet of one who brings the good news (Isaiah 52:7). The pain you may experience bringing this good news may be the vehicle God uses to bring salvation to all who believe on Jesus Christ as their Lord and Savior. Jesus knew pain and was willing to suffer and sacrifice Himself for you and me.

So why is this worth mentioning? What possible reason could this place have in our experiences in sharing Christ? Serving Christ and sharing His word of salvation is an awesome privilege. However, at times there is a required cost. The cost or pain could manifest physically, emotionally, spiritually, or mentally when approaching the hunting grounds of Satan. Paul and Silas found themselves held in the grip of suffering for the sake of the gospel, yet they emerged on this battlefield. Are we willing to go the way of Paul and Silas for the soul of others?

Pain is defined as "suffering." Synonyms for pain are discomfort, agony, torture, torment; grief, heartache, sadness and misery, just to mention a few.[8] When Paul and Silas healed the girl from her demon possession, her masters could only see revenge. The gospel meant nothing to them. All they could envision was their loss and revenge. They were angry at their loss and wanted Paul and Silas to pay, so they inflicted as much pain as they could, and it made no difference if that pain was in the form of a lie to get their desired results.

---

8   Definition of Pain in English:. (n.d.). pain: definition of pain in Oxford dictionary (American English) (US). Retrieved March 3, 2014, from http://www.oxforddictionaries.com/us/definition/american_english/pain

22

One precious thing to remember is the words of Jesus from the cross: "But Jesus was saying, 'Father, forgive them; for they do not know what they are doing.' And they cast lots, dividing up His garments among themselves" (Luke 23:34). Jesus did not excuse them. He asked God to forgive them. The pain Paul and Silas experienced had eternal results, and I am sure they would walk this same road again if the opportunity presented itself. They knew the cost but not the results. However, they stood and held no grudge, and look at what transpired:

> But about midnight Paul and Silas were praying and singing hymns of praise to God, and the prisoners were listening to them; and suddenly there came a great earthquake, so that the foundations of the prison house were shaken; and immediately all the doors were opened and everyone's chains were unfastened. When the jailer awoke and saw the prison doors opened, he drew his sword and was about to kill himself, supposing that the prisoners had escaped. But Paul cried out with a loud voice, saying, "Do not harm yourself, for we are all here!" And he called for lights and rushed in, and trembling with fear he fell down before Paul and Silas, and after he brought them out, he said, "Sirs, what must I do to be saved?" They said, "Believe in the Lord Jesus, and you will be saved, you and your household." And they spoke the word of the Lord to him together with all who were in

his house. And he took them that very hour of the night and washed their wounds, and immediately he was baptized, he and all his household. And he brought them into his house and set food before them, and rejoiced greatly, having believed in God with his whole household. (Acts 16:25–34)

This Scripture tells us that as Paul and Silas were bound to the floor of the prison, they gave praise to God through their pain, and those who were present listened (Acts 16:25). The other prisoners and guards were listening. All the praise, all the conversations, all the words of their hearts were heard by all. Wow, we stand too long in the grocery line and let the whining begin. Have you ever thought of the fact that no matter where you go, there is always someone listening and that what you say or do not say echoes through the minds of those who hear? Just when you think children are not hearing you, they come out with a profound comment and you realize they heard you.

Remember the Scripture, "Let the words of my mouth and the meditation of my heart Be acceptable in Your sight, O Lord, my rock and my Redeemer" (Psalm 19:14). No matter what the situation we find ourselves in, someone is always listening, and this too can be a tremendous witness, as demonstrated in that prison cell with Paul and Silas. What Paul and Silas suffered previously was not to compare to the joy they would soon experience. They were shackled to the prison floor and singing God's praises, and out of the blue a miracle occurred and a man and his family were about to see their whole lives change.

Remember John 16:21: "Whenever a woman is in labor she has pain, because her hour has come; but when she gives birth to the child, she no longer remembers the anguish because of the joy that a child has been born into the world." When I gave birth to my son, wow, the pain! Yet the beauty came after. Jesus in John 16 was sharing with His disciples that He was departing as He prepared for the cross and gave comfort in how their sorrow for this time would be turned to joy. Paul and Silas had experienced pain, yet out of that pain came a true blessing, and a whole family entered into the salvation of Christ. The guard knew something was missing and listened to Paul and Silas as they sang.

When our mouths open and are filled with pain indescribable, what are people hearing? When our pain is caused by another or circumstances out of our control, God can bring beauty. When our obedience is followed by the straps of pain and suffering, God can bring joy. God can bring salvation.

My younger brother went to be with the Lord at the age of fifty due to cancer. Losing him broke my heart. However, the memorial service was a part of God' salvation plan as several gave their lives to Christ. The pain my family and I suffered was the joy of those who would know Christ and His saving grace. My brother is with Jesus and now others will be also because of his witness after he died.

Pain from outside sources can open the door to God's beautiful plan. When you are going through such pain, it can be spiritually blinding, physically draining, and emotionally crippling. This pain can leave you breathless, and all sorts of feelings can find their way into your heart. What do we do in this situation? How does our witness continue when we are in pain? The answer lies in grace—God's grace. Being able to function when we are sinned against or facing our own sin is a God thing, and He alone can truly allow our witness to continue. Paul and Silas were outside the walls of prison sharing the gospel. Yet the person who would believe was found inside the prison. Although their pain was real, it did not hinder their witness. They still believed God, believed His Word, and experienced joy through praise, prayer, and God's redeeming power.

Be Prepared in Season and Out!

Paul and Silas wait in jail beaten, accused, and unsure of how their current place would pan out, yet they continued to give God the praise. The attitude they shared opened the door to salvation, and miraculous events unlike the jailer had ever seen. Only God! When we are blindsided by the pain of sharing the gospel or perhaps another area of pain, who can share an encouraging word? Who can share the plan of salvation? Witnessing is not waiting for the skies to turn blue and the sun to show its face. Only through God's amazing grace, His abounding mercy, and His endless love can we move to reach out of our pain into the pain of another.

This is a note worth pondering: when I am at my lowest, someone will almost always wander into my path, and that someone will need the Savior. At the most miserable times we can imagine, there they are lost and needing the good news of the gospel. We reason in ourselves, "The timing is all wrong. God, I am hurting. Why are You bringing this person to me now?" Paul and Silas were hurting. They had every reason to shut their eyes to all the events going on around them, yet when those doors swung open, all they saw was opportunity.

Why would God bring a lost soul into my life when I am at my lowest with so much pain? The Scripture tells us to be ready in season and out of season to share the good news. Perhaps our pain opens a door that no one else can open. Perhaps to make the most of this place means seeing the pain of another going past our own. No one else at that moment may be able to reach through the present pain quite the way you could.

During 9/11, many people were hurt, confused, devastated, and lost. The images are forever planted in our memories of those running and confused at the horror of that day. Yet many gave sacrificially to help those whose pain was greater than their own. No one asked to be at that place at that time. However, many sailed above the noise of their own pain to reach the hurting around them. Making the most of the place they found themselves, many who felt the dagger of pain themselves chose to reach out to those who were hurting as well. During one of the most horrendous days in US history, many chose to reach out to others by reaching past their own pain to help others. Through the anguish salvation came to many in the face of those who would sacrifice so others might live.

God can be seen in the deepest pain, and the doors of opportunity can bust wide open even in the hands of chaos. First Peter 3:15 says, "but sanctify Christ as Lord in your hearts, always being ready to make a defense to everyone who asks you to give an account for the hope that is in you, yet with gentleness and reverence." Being a hope bringer is a tremendous responsibility.

Things aren't always neat and tidy. Opportunity does not always knock when the house is clean. No matter what state we may find ourselves in, God can use this place we dwell in at this moment and make something fantastic flow from the depths of our lives. Remember that someone else may listen and hear the voice of God as He shares through Christ His plan for salvation no matter what our circumstances may be.

How It Works!

Do you know that Christ died for your sins and mine? *Do* you know that in the midst of His great sorrow and pain, He remembered you? *Do* you know that *God* loves you no matter what state you are in? *Do* you know? *Do* you remember the place of your life before Jesus saved you? It does not matter where you were; it matters where you are now. If you need Christ as your personal Savior, now is the time. John 3:16 says, "For God so loved the world that He gave His only Son that who so ever believes in Him should not perish but have ever lasting life." Ask Jesus into your life today. There is more about this at the end of the book. You know many Christians never come to the place of sharing their faith. If you are a living daily for Christ Christian, you will want to lead people to Him and make the most of the place you are in right now. These are just ideas to perhaps encourage your journey.

1. First, learn to share God's plan of salvation or stay tuned in and in shape to share the gospel. Our church at the present time as a body of Christ is going through the *Billy Graham:*

Christian Life and Witness Course.[9] Find fresh ideas for sharing the gospel. Remember, the message never changes; however, the method may. One of my favorite places to go is online is called The Way of the Master, hosted by Ray Comfort and Kirk Cameron.[10] You can find nearly any answer to your questions here. They capture sharing the gospel in a magnificent way. You can watch videos that show and explain sharing the gospel in many areas of life. Both give a 100 percent when sharing the gospel. Let's face it, many of us now live in totally different family dynamics, and with the growth of blended families and our ever-changing society, we need unique ways to share the gospel. This website shares some of these ways. Other places to search are your church library, your pastor's office (please don't tell him I said so), Christian bookstores, and Sunday school teachers. Another website would be Billy Graham. org.[11] The resources are endless. Do study the website you choose and explore it to make sure the gospel is represented by the death, burial, and resurrection of Christ and that He alone is "the way, the truth and the life" (John 14:6). Remember, though, the greatest resources are the Holy Spirit and God's Word.

---

9   Christian life and witness course (Rev. ed.). (Minneapolis, MN: Billy Graham Evangelistic Association, 1999).

10 The Way of the Master. (n.d.). The Way of the Master. Retrieved March 23, 2014, from http://www.wayofthemaster.com/index.shtml

11 Grow Your Faith. (n.d.). Billy Graham Evangelistic Association. Retrieved March 23, 2014, from http://billygraham.org/grow-your-faith/

2. Second, pray for the lost people in your life by name. Ask God to provide an opportunity to share the gospel. It will come. But start with learning the gospel and how to share first. It may take a few times of witnessing before the truth makes its way to their hearts. Be patient. This is God's work, and He controls the outcome and results. We are told to "go and preach the gospel and make disciples" (Matthew 28:19–20).

3. Third, understand a cost may be required. Do not shrink from this responsibility. God will be honored, and God will bless your efforts. Remember the words of Jesus in Luke 14. Jesus spoke about the cost of discipleship in verses 27 through 29. Giving Jesus our all, being prepared in and out of season, and weighing the cost of discipleship are how we start to share the gospel so others can join the march of the saints. Paul and Silas had no idea what was to come, yet they were ready. Do you want to have victory in this area of your life and make the most of this place? After you have taken the steps to better serve our Lord, pray as you release the praise for God to empower you to share His beautiful plan of salvation with a lost world. He will!

Fourth, don't be afraid. I remember the first time I shared the gospel. It was at a backyard Bible club in New Jersey. I had shared with a group of children how God loved them and Jesus paid the price for their sins. A number of children asked Jesus to be their Savior. As I took one of the children to her mom, we shared with the mother the decision that had been made. The mom appeared to be disappointed. I ask if she was all right, and she said no one had ever shared Jesus with her. So I did, and she asked the Lord to be her Savior. All I had to do was trust the Holy Spirit to lead, and salvation came to this mom and her daughter. Trust, plan, and then prayerfully share how Christ has changed your life.

"God is always working around us. Those who are sensitive to His ways will rejoice with Him and join Him in His work. In doing so, He opens our eyes to the needs around us, then empowers us to meet the needs". [12]

Dave Earley and David Wheeler

---

12 D. Earley & D. A. Wheeler (2010). Evangelism is: Not Following the Example of the Disciples. Evangelism is--: how to share Jesus with passion and confidence (p. 131). Nashville, Tenn.: B & H Academic.

Chapter 3

The Place of Conflict

If you share a home with at least one other person, you know conflict. Conflict is a part of life. It can be short and sweet or long and brutal. Is conflict good, bad, or even necessary? What causes conflict? Should I try to live my life conflict free? These questions are worth the study. Paul and Silas met their conflict and perhaps answered some of these questions.

Paul and Silas knew conflict. They did not go looking for it, yet there they were right in the middle of a full-blown conflict. Their conflict began when she, a walking and talking conflict, began to follow Paul and Silas around town, shouting who they were and what they were all about. This conflict was so loud that Paul in his irritation spoke to the conflict in the name of Jesus, and the conflict came out. Not only was the conflict inside this girl, but the conflict overflowed into the lives of Paul and Silas. Although the conflict within the girl was now taken care of, the conflict outside grew. Paul solved one conflict, but it was replaced by another.

We need to understand how conflict is defined and how conflict works. Conflict means "a serious disagreement or argument … a prolonged armed struggle." Synonyms for conflict are dispute, quarrel, squabble, disagreement, dissension, clash; discord, friction, strife, antagonism, hostility, disputation, contention; feud, and schism.[13] After we read such a description, we wonder how conflict could ever weigh healthy in people's lives, much less their walks with the Lord. However, when handled properly, scripturally, and prayerfully, conflict can resolve pending and perhaps future issues. Conflict can represent good or bad.

Conflict will come whether we want it or not. It's like a toothache—nagging and painful, and it is not going away unless it is dealt with. The toothache reveals something is wrong and the issue of aching needs to be addressed. Conflict can be handled a number of ways, and by the time you finish this chapter, perhaps conflict will take on a different shape and open your eyes to your own resolve.

It makes no difference whether it is the workplace, church, a retail store, an office building, or a restaurant or in the family dynamics. Conflict happens. Why? Simply put, people. People bring conflict purposely and unknowingly. Conflict happens for such reasons as we see in the synonyms just mentioned. Dispute,

---

13 Definition of Conflict in English:. (n.d.). Conflict: definition of conflict in Oxford dictionary (American English) (US). Retrieved March 23, 2014, from http://www.oxforddictionaries.com/us/definition

quarrel, squabble, disagreement—all give place to one person wanting his or her way and another wanting his or her way. Dissension, clash, discord, friction, strife, antagonism, hostility, disputation, contention, feud, and schism all give way to friction that begins within a person and overflows to the next.

Check out James 4:1–3. When two opposing sides decide that their way or idea is better … conflict. The next thing you, know a spark ignites and everyone is yelling, "Fire." Get out of the way before you get burned. You know how it goes. There's a family gathering and Uncle Bob says to Aunt Mary, "Put on a little weight, I see." Well, Aunt Mary has to come back with, "Well, I see your hair has bid you farewell," and the conflict has begun. This may appear simple enough. However, many a family or business partners have split over much less. Conflict happens when self gets in the way and causes a collision. A serious wreck is about to happen unless proper measures are taken. Look at some of these places where conflict may erupt.

One of the greatest areas of conflict is the workplace. Having been in retail management for nearly forty years and church ministry for nearly thirty-five years, I have seen the ugly and healthy side of conflict. Competition in the workplace for status, money, and the boss's eye has proven many times over to be the end of friendships, reputations, and careers. Competition when applied respectfully can prove to be a great motivator. However, when selfish ambition clouds the vision, right judgment flies out the window and full-scale assault and conflict arise, and the picture is not a pretty one.

When we revisit Acts 16, we see that the men who owned the girl became angered at Paul and Silas not because they stirred up trouble in the town as accused. The conflict occurred when these men realized that without the girl, they were out of business. This was the root of the conflict: loss of revenue. And many times this is true today. The competition for money and the like is like two female lions fighting for supper. Someone's going to get hurt. For many of us, the workplace is where we have to be to earn our living, whether we desire this place or not. And depending on the place and the number of people involved, the area of conflict can be quite explosive at times. For some you shy away from the conflict. For others conflict becomes explosive, neither of which solves a thing. The workplace brings with it a host of conflicts, which we can use to grow in ourselves or encourage another in growth. It is all in how one responds and receives during a particular conflict.

Another place of conflict is seen in the family. The role of the family has changed dramatically over the last few years, and conflict is taking on a whole new face. One such family is the blended family. A blended family is defined as, "A family consisting of a couple, the children they have had together, and their children from previous relationships."[14] Although many families blended or not, have good family relations, this is not always the case. Like with the story of Paul and Silas in Acts 16 and in our own families, it seems that when people think they are losing something or

---

14 Definition of Blended Family in English: (n.d.). Blended family: definition of blended family in Oxford dictionary (British & World English). Retrieved April 6, 2014, from http://www.oxforddictionaries.com/definition/english/blended-family.

someone, conflict erupts. In Paul's case it was the loss of money. Families today are faced with ongoing issues that seek to rip away a family's foundation. These conflicts demonstrate themselves in the lack of fiancés, jobs, health care, you name it. The family is facing numerous areas that have increased conflict in the home. Lack of responsibility, selfishness, and giving are other areas that seem to light the way to conflict. Conflict has attacked many family structures. The blended family is just one example.

The church has not been exempt from the area of conflict. With families feeling the weight of society, such as growing economic issues, the church overflows with conflict and is performing more repair work than ever. Helping families in crisis and conflict is a growing concern among our churches, or at least it should be. In our churches the area of control can be a conflicting topic. Pastors all over the world can attest to this. Whether the control comes from government, community, or even their own church members, control can lead to explosive conflict that can split a church apart.

One point needed here when addressing conflict in our lives, no matter where it may come from, is that our source of guidance should start with God's Holy Word. This counsel is the place of discovery that helps us move in the right direction. As mentioned before, conflict can be bad and good.

One last place of conflict that we will look at and is of the most importance is that of the cross. When Christ was hung on the cross, a conflict ensued between light and dark. This conflict was won, however, with Jesus' death and resurrection. Jesus knew the conflict was there, yet He stayed the course, never resorted to violence, and allowed the Father's will to prevail. What a Savior we have. The cross provides an example of love winning over conflict. The cross is the greatest example of conflict and how this conflict was necessary for all humanity.

Learning and Need

Conflict happens, yet it can result in resolved issues. Conflict has its place, and as mentioned before conflict, can assist in unraveling unforeseen issues and lingering issues. As with Paul and Silas, they had no idea that releasing this girl from her demon would cause such an issue. Notice they did not run, back down, or cave in to fear no matter what the accusation. They did not try to demand they were right. They did not explode with unbridled anger either.

Our response matters. Paul and Silas were willing to forgo any retaliation to allow God to work. In other words, they did not have to be right. They did not have to have the last word; they trusted God and waited for His guidance. Hard, sure, yet worth the wait.

> But when her masters saw that their hope of profit was gone, they seized Paul and Silas and dragged them into the market place before the authorities, and when they had brought them to the chief magistrates, they said, "These men are throwing our city into confusion, being Jews, and are proclaiming customs which it is not lawful for us to accept or to observe, being Romans. (Acts 16:19–21).

medal. Prayerfully, respectfully applying God's Word will help begin the process of healing (Ephesians 5:1–21).

3. Remember, there are two sides to the story. Both believe they are right. Include a trusted third party, like a pastor or workplace counselor, to help unresolved issues. Never make your conflict with another common gossip; this will hurt your chances of reconciliation (Matthew 5:23–24).

4. Look for a God-centered reason for the conflict. Is God trying to reveal a wrong attitude, unconfessed sin, or perhaps the need of another that may not have revealed itself without the conflict? Pray for insight into the conflict that God may be trying to reveal to you (Psalm 119:71). A word: this is not seeking out conflict or afflicting yourself or making yourself a victim to gain answers; this is going through life and allowing God to reveal His will to you when conflict comes.

5. Practice reflective practices and praying. Don't always assume that the problem lies with the other person. A great read is *Standards-Based Reflective Practice* by Elizabeth Spalding, Jesus Garcia, and Joseph A. Braun.[15] Although this book is geared toward teaching methods, it is a wonderful book to encourage reflective practices that help in all walks of life (Acts 10).

6. When you are involved in conflict where the other person will not listen to reason, remain calm. Do not retaliate or

---

15 E. Spalding, Garcia, J., & Braun, J. A. *Standards-Based Reflective Practice: An introduction to standards-based reflective practice for middle and high school teaching.* (New York: Teachers College Press, 2010).

use frontal confrontation. Wait for the right timing. Pray and ask God to help you find a solution (Psalm 40:17). In a church function one day, I unknowing offended a fellow church member. I did not find out from the person offended. I found out through a third party. I approached the offended party, and she insisted I had meant to offend her and promised never to forgive me. She was true to her word. That was thirty years ago, and now that person harbors a bitter spirit. I lamented over this for a long time and came to realize that I had asked for forgiveness a number of times, from my Lord and the person. Now I must move on, knowing that God has it under control.

7. Don't run from the conflict. Remember, conflict can help reveal a need. So listen and let God guide you through the conflict so you can learn what needs may be present. And then act in a godly manner (Nehemiah 4). Always use God's wisdom and caution in and during conflict. Walking away is always an option and is best when things get heated. When the other party is unwilling to work on the problem, walk away and give it prayer and time. God will open the door when the time is right.

8. When you know there is conflict begin with prayer and seeking God's face. You will find this is always the best way. Allow time. Most conflicts need time to resolve (Proverbs 3:5, 6).

9. Do not allow pride to stand in the way of peace (Proverbs 11:2).

Ask yourself what is the real reason for the conflict, and direct those reasons to Scripture for a solution (Psalm 119). Keep Christ at the center of all your solutions.

"If you're in a difficult place right now, perhaps you need to entrust the problem to the Lord and leave it in His hands awhile. He alone can storm the impregnable, devise the improbable, and perform the impossible".[16]

R. J. Morgan

We are in this together. Conflict is a part of life, but it need not tear your life apart. Think about it.

---

16   R. J. Morgan (2001). Waiting. The Red Sea rules: 10 God-given strategies for difficult times (p. 51). Nashville: T. Nelson.

Chapter 4

The Place of Self

There is a great website called random acts of kindness.org. Perhaps you have heard of it.[17] This website has designated its spaces to reporting the wonderful acts of kindness done by people of all ages. Now why in the world would I share this first when this chapter is titled "The Place of Self"? This is easy to answer. When one is focused on demonstrating kind acts to another, self has no place. Have you ever just picked up a dictionary and read the words that come after self? Self is defined "to, with, for, or toward oneself or itself."[18] There is self-willed, self-centered, self-denied, and the list

---

17   Welcome | Random Acts of Kindness. (n.d.). Welcome | Random Acts of Kindness. Retrieved April 12, 2014, from http://www.randomactsofkindness.org/

18   "Definition of Self in English." self: definition of self in Oxford dictionary (British & World English). N.p., n.d. Web. 10 Aug. 2014. http://www.oxforddictionaries.com/definition

goes on to about eighty-five different definitions to follow self. Our view of self makes a huge difference on our outlook and where we place our importance. The place of self is like cotton candy. Man is it sweet, yet given too much time and space and what a mess it creates.

Paul and Silas were the main focus at the beginning of the book. However, now we will look to several others: the owners of the possessed girl and those who threw Paul and Silas in jail, the chief magistrates.

> But when her masters saw that their hope of profit was gone, they seized Paul and Silas and dragged them into the market place before the authorities, and when they had brought them to the chief magistrates, they said, "These men are throwing our city into confusion, being Jews, and are proclaiming customs which it is not lawful for us to accept or to observe, being Romans. (Acts 16:19–21)

Notice the first line: "But when her masters saw that their hope of profit was gone they seized Paul and Silas and dragged them into the market place before the authorities." Their profit was gone. Self had been denied, and now someone would pay a dear price. No matter what you call it—entitlement, self-pursuit, worked for, it's my turn now—when it becomes all about self, someone always gets hurt. Attitudes change, purposes get clouded, and visions fade. Had Christ wanted to spare Himself the agony of the cross, you and I would be lost for eternity and forever separated from our heavenly Father.

The Scriptures can refer to self as not so good, as found in Matthew 23:25: "Woe to you, scribes and Pharisees, hypocrites! For you clean the outside of the cup and of the dish, but inside they are full of robbery and *self-indulgence.*" Second Timothy 3:2 (referring to the last days) says, "For men will be *lovers of self,* lovers of money, boastful, arrogant, revilers, disobedient to parents, ungrateful, unholy." Yet the Scripture speaks about practicing self-control or selflessness as being a positive venture (Galatians 5:22–24, Romans 15:1). We all know the act of selfishness or self-centeredness. Look at the chief magistrates:

> The crowd rose up together against them, and the chief magistrates tore their robes off them and proceeded to order them to be beaten with rods. When they had struck them with many blows, they threw them into prison, commanding the jailer to guard them securely; and he, having received such a command, threw them into the inner prison and fastened their feet in the stocks. (Acts 16:22–24)

These guys thought they were doing the right thing. Remember in conflict everyone thinks his or her way is the right way. When a person battles self-righteousness, the rightness always appears to be theirs. However, as we see the events unfold, the magistrate realize what a mistake had been made:

Now when day came, the chief magistrates sent their policemen, saying, "Release those men." And the jailer reported these words to Paul, saying, "The chief magistrates have sent to release you. Therefore come out now and go in peace." But what the magistrate fails to realize is that Paul is about to unfold the truth and they were about to get very nervous. But Paul said to them, "They have beaten us in public without trial, men who are Romans, and have thrown us into prison; and now are they sending us away secretly? No indeed! But let them come themselves and bring us out." The policemen reported these words to the chief magistrates. They were afraid when they heard that they were Romans, and they came and appealed to them, and when they had brought them out, they kept begging them to leave the city. They went out of the prison and entered the house of Lydia, and when they saw the brethren, they encouraged them and departed. (Acts 16:35–40)

Now what in the world does this have to do with self, and shouldn't this be in the conflict section? Hang on … remember when Paul and Silas were arrested, they were accused: "And when they had brought them to the chief magistrates, they said, 'These men are throwing our city into confusion, being Jews, and are claiming customs which it is not lawful for us to accept or to ve, being Romans'" (Acts 16:20–21). And now the magistrates find out they were Romans. Without finding out the truth, these men believed other men and created another problem—they had punished Roman citizens, and their self-righteousness had gotten them in a whole lot of trouble. And to top it off, Paul said, "Now wait a minute. You have beaten us, jailed us, and humiliated us, and now want to dismiss us privately. No way. You come and take us out so everyone can see the mistake that was made." Paul, without attacking, stood his ground and faced his accusers.

When people act in a selfish manner, they later may try to excuse themselves. Selfishness works this way. Owning our mistakes makes it easy to find forgiveness. The person who has been offended in respect and led by the Lord communicates that this behavior is unacceptable to perhaps prevent the same event in the future.

Selfish acts and lack of information can indeed cause major problems and must be handled in a godly manner to accomplish the desired results. So the opening part of this chapter makes sense, does it not? Putting others first and acting out in kindness make more sense. Being giving people goes against our nature (Colossians 3:9–11). Yet in Christ we can do the impossible. We can help self-take a backseat and even like it.

My son, while in college, dressed like the Chick-fil-a cow at half time in college to make some extra funds (the picture hangs in my study), and as a result he made some little children very happy. He was so good at this, and I am sure got quite the ribbing from friends, yet he laid self aside and jumped out there to brighten up lives. His wife and my daughter-in-law, is the same way. She gives to help others in their walk in life. They are willing to lay self aside to make a difference in the lives of others.

Many others in my family and yours have done the same. Church members, pastors, missionaries, neighbors, politicians, teachers, police, firemen, nurses, mechanics, retail and wholesale merchants, workers of all kinds, moms, dads, brothers, sisters, and our military have with many others sacrificed for the welfare of others. These selfless acts are what bring unity, joy, peace, healing, encouragement, love, and sacrifice. Having this kind of attitude is what makes our country stand apart and makes us different. Selfishness, self-centeredness, and the like are what rip the seam right out of the garment. What may take a great deal of time to build with love and respect only takes a second to fall when attacked with the ugliness of selfishness.

Recognize

When Paul and Silas cast out the demon from the girl, they were in for a whole lot of self-motivated problems from her owners. They made up lies to dress the truth and would not stop until these two were locked up tight. In our society today, many believe that self is what life is all about. What makes me happy, what I can get for me, what do I get out of it, how can this benefit me, and I am entitled are the actions of some yet should never be in the heart of the Christian.

We as Christians are entitled only because of what Christ did on the cross. His shed blood brought salvation. His finished work brings us to heaven, and His sacrifice opens the door to the throne. Christ and His selfless act bring salvation. Paul and Silas experienced the owner of this possessed girl's wrath. Their selfish act brought havoc to the lives of Paul and Silas. Yet God, as mentioned throughout this book, is in charge.

Actually when you think about it, Paul and Silas could have been showing mercy to this girl. Perhaps when she followed them and called out, she was not enhancing their mission.[19] Who knows how long she had been used by these men and bore this burden. She was now free, and Paul and Silas would bear the burden. It seems that the last place we look to when self gets in the way is at ourselves. When we face this kind of opposition, we are quick to become defensive. Yet Paul and Silas remained calm and allowed God to work, which revealed a deeper need.

When you find yourself at the end of any self-centered attack from another, recognize where this attack comes from. These men who depended on this girl for funds were not empowered by God. They were influenced by the prince of this world and the influence of money and self. This threesome is very destructive, but be encouraged—you have a greater team on your side if you have the Lord Jesus as your Savior. God the Father, God the Son, and God the Holy Spirit—man, what a team. Wow, this is quite a revelation that you have such a team in the battle and fighting the battle for you. Remember what Jesus said in John 16:33: "These things I have spoken to you, so that in Me you may have peace. In the world you have tribulation, but take courage; I have overcome the world." Self can hinder the greatest of Christians. Yet it need

19   N. T. Wright *Acts for Everyone*. (Louisville, KY: Westminster John Knox Press, 2008), E-book.

not stay this way. How we choose to behave is solely up to us. Would you like to know the secret to a Christ-centered life versus a self-centered life?

Stay Humble

Okay, some people just went off, and the word humility is to blame. Whatever you have been taught, humility is not weakness, self-condemning, or being brutal to one's self. Humility from the Scripture's point of view can be found in John 13 when Jesus washed the feet of His disciples. What He was trying to get across was to serve one another and humble yourself to help others.[20] As the scripture tells us, "Do nothing from selfishness or empty conceit, but with humility of mind regard one another as more important than yourselves" (Philippians 2:3). The men who owned this girl in Acts 16 must not have been in church on the Sunday this was preached. Recognize that the selfish motives of another are not of God. The god of this world (2 Corinthians 4:3–5) has blinded people and seeks to cause confusion and chaos. Recognize that God wants His children to give themselves for the benefit of others. Recognize that the reward of putting others first is developing the mind of Christ, encouraging another, assisting in helping a fellow man, and teaching our children and their children respect and true love, which over flows into all relationships. Recognize that there will always be someone who lives for self,

---

20 M. J. Erickson, *Christian Theology* (2nd ed.). (Grand Rapids, MI: Baker Book House, 1998), (p.131).

but this does not need to be you. The Scripture also raises the bar a bit more for His children. Read how God sees the humble:

Psalm 25:9 says, "He leads the humble in justice, And He teaches the humble His way." Proverbs 29:23 says, "A man's pride will bring him low, But a humble spirit will obtain honor." Zephaniah 2:3 says, "Seek the Lord, All you humble of the earth Who have carried out His ordinances; Seek righteousness, seek humility. Perhaps you will be hidden In the day of the Lord's anger." Jesus spoke about this subject as well in Matthew 11:29: "Take My yoke upon you and learn from Me, for I am gentle and humble in heart, and you will find rest for your souls." Matthew 18:4 says, "Whoever then humbles himself as this child, he is the greatest in the kingdom of heaven." Having a humble mind and spirit does not make you weak or cowardly. On the contrary, it takes courage, supernatural strength, and Holy Spirit power to walk this path. If you want to see a perfect example of strength, courage, and humility, look at the cross of Jesus. The cross explains it all. Paul and Silas responded to these men with humility, honor, and strength. Paul and Silas knew who was really in charge, and they were able to find rest, peace, and song amid it all.

How It Works!

1. Resolve yourself to practice Romans 12:3: "For through the grace given to me I say to everyone among you not to think more highly of himself than he ought to think; but to think so as to have sound judgment, as God has allotted to each a measure of faith." The kindness website mentioned

earlier has wonderful stories of giving and selflessness and may be a start to help us become a more caring people. This is a difficult step, but understand that this step moves mountains. Let Christ be your example of love and giving to another.

2. Recognize that not all will agree with this part of the book. Some argue, "I work hard for what I have." Others will say, "No one does for me." These responses have been addressed at the beginning of the chapter. You can walk a life designed to bless others, and I know you want to. Remember, as a Christian you are on the winning side. You may suffer at another's selfishness, but you need not fall into the same place. Be understanding. Be resolved. Practice a giving heart. Acts 20:35 says, "In everything I showed you that by working hard in this manner you must help the weak and remember the words of the Lord Jesus, that He Himself said, 'It is more blessed to give than to receive.'"

3. Begin to reach out in your own home, community, church, or workplace, and be that selfless person who starts a fire of kindness. It can be as small as a ride to work or as big as watching some kids. You can do it. Resolve to follow the example of Christ with a self-giving life.

If you have found that you are indeed in the place of self, stop here and ask God to help you out. He will! This is one of the unhappiest places you will ever find yourself. So ask God right now to move you to step out of the place of self.

"One of the reasons we struggle so much is because while the world is feeding the old nature, the new nature is being starved to death. We have put it on a low calorie diet".[21]

David Jeremiah

---

21 D. Jeremiah (1995). Study Guide, the Work of the Flesh and the Fruit of the Spirit. The fruit of the Spirit (p. 13). Atlanta, Ga.: Walk Through the Bible Ministries.

Chapter 5

The Place of Defeat

Have you ever been bungee jumping? For some this is a thrill. However, for the rest this is fear unbridled. Lying about your weight in this situation may not be a good idea. How about hang gliding? Ever felt the need to jump off a cliff and glide to the ground with ease? These and perhaps a few other areas seem to be only for the thrill seeker, yet we all dream of the courage these "fun" adventures must take. Jumping off a bridge and plunging to the ground below with only a short rope would take a bit of courage for some of us. Challenging is an understatement.

What is the most challenging place you have ever found yourself? Have you ever been in a small room filled with two- and three-year-old little girls? For some this is magic, yet others would need therapy after the fact. Victory would not be their battle cry.

Perhaps your challenge is just getting up in the morning. Is your challenge one that you would never mention out loud? You've done your best and cannot seem to reach the mountaintop. Giving all you have only to face discouragement and feelings of defeat is no victory at all, some may say.

Think on that for a minute. Have you ever given 110 percent, only to find your efforts were fruitless? Perhaps like me you have taken a test and missed it by one point. Or perhaps you auditioned for that top part only to find yourself in second place; me too. Maybe at work you have worked on an idea that took months to prepare, only to see your efforts slip into the hands of another. Or maybe you have tried every diet out there, only to have your efforts fail time and time again; I have. It is like jumping from a plane with no parachute or off a cliff with the people calculating the rope thinking you weigh 120 pounds when in reality you weigh 200.

This chapter is for those of us who have felt or do feel defeated. Life has you in a paper bag and with a big stick is having its way with you. You know the place. Maybe you lost a job lately and have been out looking for a new job. This can be brutal and defeating. But hold on, you need not remain in this place.

How do you define defeat? Many people add their own definition to the word *defeat*; however, Oxford Dictionary defines the word this way: to win a battle over (someone or something) in a war, contest, game, etc., to cause (someone or something) to fail, to control or overcome (something).[22] What is your definition?

---

22 "Definition of Defeat in English." Defeat: definition of defeat in Oxford dictionary (British & World English). N.p., n.d. Web. 10 Aug. 2014. <http://www.oxforddictionaries.com/definition

What some may view as defeat God views as victorious—for example, the cross. To those who hung Jesus on the cross, He was defeated and at His end. However, God saw His sacrifice as salvation for the sins of the world (Romans 5:8). God sees victory in places we would never dream.

Paul and Silas in prison would not seem like a victory to most. The jailer in Acts 16 at a certain point felt defeated and as a result thought taking his life was the best answer. This is never true. Acts 16:27 says, "When the jailer awoke and saw the prison doors opened, he drew his sword and was about to kill himself, supposing that the prisoners had escaped." Remember with self, getting the wrong impression or information can lead to the wrong conclusion.

We see this same scenario once more. When we begin to go inward, we can often make the wrong assumption. What we see as a failure, an end, or defeat may be a door that God is developing in another direction. Our reaction to the events may very well be the determining factor to how that door opens. An earthquake shakes the place, the doors swing open, and the guard assumes all have escaped. This thought almost cost him his life, yet Paul was ready to encourage.

You see, Paul envisioned more than a failure; he viewed an opportunity. Picture this: Paul is beaten and chained to the floor, along with Silas. Paul calls out to this jailer, who figures all is lost, to save his life. The jailer rushes in and falls before them, wanting to know how to be saved. Even though this man was the enemy at the moment, Paul saw him as a brother in the making. Paul reached out in the jailer's defeated state and touched his life to give him purpose and meaning. We can look past a seemingly defeated moment and become a Paul or Silas for someone or perhaps the jailer. God has a victory to uncover and bring you and me past the moment of defeat.

Perhaps the place you feel this defeat is your marriage, children, health, church, or workplace. No matter where your defeat package comes from, you can have victory. Remember in the Christians life there are no coincidences, only God's divine purpose (Jeremiah 29:11). Let me say first I have no idea where your victory will come from or how. I do know the author of victory, and He is always ready to help. "God is our refuge and strength, a very *present help* in trouble" (Psalm 46:1).

Hang On!

What I do not want to focus so much on is the defeat you may be carrying as I do your victory. God desires you and me to be victorious. Do you believe this? Zephaniah 3:17 says, "The Lord your God is with you, the Mighty Warrior who saves. He will take great delight in you; in His love He will no longer rebuke you, but will rejoice over you with singing" (NIV).

If you are reading this and are overwhelmed with defeat, you need not stay at this place. And the answer is the voice of one calling your name to hang on. Christ knows your name, and He wants you to stop, listen, and believe. Look at the jailer and Paul's interaction. The jailer was about to end it all because it appeared hopeless and defeating. However, watch Paul in verse 28: "But

Paul cried out with a loud voice, saying, 'Do not harm yourself, for we are all here!'"

Notice what Paul did first; he cried out with a loud voice. "While he could see nothing as he looked into the darkness, those inside could see his figure silhouetted in the doorway and could see what he was about to do."[23] Paul's cry saved the man. I am not sure where you are but the voice of God is calling you, perhaps to salvation, perhaps to ministry, perhaps to wait, rest, or move. Wherever you find your place, be aware that defeat can easily meet you at the door if you let it. What and who you choose to believe is the difference. Had the jailer failed to listen to the voice that called out to him in the darkness, he would have gone into eternity without Christ.

If you feel defeated, stop here and read Genesis 16. Hagar was Sara's maid, ready to have Abraham's child. Sara and Hagar had a conflict. Hagar escaped, only to find defeat as her only companion. In the middle of the battle, and defeat is a battle, God appeared. Remember, He is a "present help" in times of trouble. After He called out to Hagar, she made this statement in verse 13: "Then she called the name of the Lord who spoke to her, 'You are a God who sees.'"

The jailer had no idea what was going on. However, one thing is for sure: the ground was not the only thing shaken. Paul cried out that everyone was there. Verses 29 and 30 say, "And he called for lights and rushed in, and trembling with fear he fell down before Paul and Silas, and after he brought them out, he said, 'Sirs,

---

23 F. F. Bruce, *The Book of the Acts* (Rev. Ed.). (Grand Rapids, MI: William B. Eerdmans Publishing Co., 1988), (p.317).

what must I do to be saved?'" He could hardly believe it; they were all accounted for.

What you choose to believe and the voice you choose to hear will determine where you end up. The jailer chose to hear Paul's voice, and as a result salvation came to his home. What voices are screaming in your ear? Remember the wife of Job (Job 2:9–10). It is a good thing Job choose not to listen to this voice of defeat. As this book has evolved, the one thing that has remained constant is that God is faithful. Just when you think all is lost, there He is in the middle holding your hand and lifting you up. Listen to His voice in the middle of your circumstances, not the voice of defeat.

Remember what was taking place during the worship service in the jail cell. All were listening (verse 25). That means anyone who was present heard the worship and praise, and that would mean the jailer. The jailer had witnessed praise in tribulation, praise through pain, and praise in the most unlikely place. The jailer had witnessed the miracle of the doors being opened and the miracle when not one prisoner escaped. Therefore when the jailer chose to believe, salvation came to his home. Now what about you and me? Are we in a place of defeat? Are we hanging on or hanging out? Is the rope getting slippery? Hang on! There is hope. We have a very pleasant help in times of trouble.

Listen to the Right Voice!

Remember the voice we talked about briefly, the one of defeat or victory. Let me dig a bit deeper. The voice you listen to can make or break you, literally. Be picky about the voice calling your name. Is defeat calling your name and proclaiming that you are nothing and you can do nothing? Hang up the phone. Turn off the text, and shut down the Internet. That is utter hogwash. Christ died for you, and that makes you special. Christ suffered for you. That made you worth it. Right now decide you are no longer going to give place to the voices of those who would imprison you in your thoughts.

Know this: every defeated place you find yourself begins in your thoughts. When you are sitting in the darkness, whose voice are you going to listen to? Don't let the voice of confusion, doubt, and despair, which belongs to Satan our accuser (Revelation 12:10), keep you from hearing the voice of truth, which is the Lord Jesus Christ. "We overcome the accuser of our brothers and sisters, we overcome our consciences, we overcome our bad tempers, we overcome our defeats, we overcome our lusts, we overcome our fears, we overcome our pettiness on the basis of the blood of the Lamb"[24]

When you belong to Christ, His voice is the voice to follow, and we should follow His voice alone. Doing this means getting to know His voice by listening. This happens by reading, studying, and applying His Word to our daily walks and continual prayers. Sheep know their master's voice, and they will run away from a stranger. So it is with the voice of Jesus.

> Therefore Pilate said to Him, "So You are a king?"
> Jesus answered, "You say correctly that I am a king.

---

24 D. A. Carson (2010). Scandalous: the cross and resurrection of Jesus. Wheaton, Ill.: Crossway. E book.

For this I have been born, and for this I have come
into the world, to testify to the truth. Everyone who
is of the truth hears My voice." (John 18:37)

Challenge the voice that calls your name. Make sure it is
Christ and not the accuser. The accuser will use any means and
anyone to keep you defeated. Do not stay in this place. Remember
conflict? Here you go. In all of us there is this conflict of thoughts.
Make them subject to Christ (2 Corinthians 10:5). Tough? Sure.
However, the reward is priceless: peace of mind and victory.

One area where destructive voices can invade thoughts is seen
over and over again in abusive relationships. The abuser often
voices the unworthiness of the abused. If you are in an abusive
relationship, seek help from a professional counselor. Don't believe
you can handle this alone. Get help. Learning to listen to the
proper voice comes when we have given our lives to Christ and we
realize our worth through Him. Defeated? No way. Like Paul said,
"But we have this treasure in earthen vessels, so that the surpassing
greatness of the power will be of God and not from ourselves;
we are afflicted in every way, but not crushed; perplexed, but not
despairing; persecuted, but not forsaken; struck down, but not
destroyed" (2 Corinthians 4:7–9). There are times we feel defeated
but we won't stay in this place, right?

How It Works!

There are steps you can take when you find yourself in the place of defeat:

1. Be able to identify the place you feel defeated. Is it physical, emotional, or spiritual? This is an important step. When people are facing physical challenges, they can receive false signals. Physical problems can deceive you into thinking you are defeated when this is not the case at all. Check with your physician and be honest about how you feel. Remember, God knows what's going on, so trust Him to be that "present help." Once you have determined whether the problem is physical or in another area, you can move on from there.

2. Remember to make a prayerful effort to listen to the right voice. Study God's Word to learn the Father's voice. Commit His Word to your life and memory, to your thoughts. Let His thoughts be yours. Remember, God is not defeated, but Satan is (Revelation 12:9, 20:2). God is right there beside us, as He promised (Hebrews 13:5). Develop a prayer closet. This is where we go to get our daily supply of strength, mercy, grace, forgiveness, ideas, hope, joy, self-control, vision, perhaps some answers, God's promises, and a laugh or two. Yes, I am serious. God and I laugh all the time at some of the things I do and say. He has a tremendous sense of humor. This is where I remember what I have forgotten about God and who He is. My closet

is a favorite chair in my living room at 3:00 every morning. God is always there to meet me and I with Him.

3. If you are in an abusive relationship, physical, emotional, or verbal, get help! Do not try to go this road alone. There are places to turn. You are not defeated. If you have a church, seek out your pastor. If you do not have a church, go to http://www.thehotline.org, 1-800-799-SAFE (7233). Don't wait. Listen to the voice of truth. There is a heavenly Father who wants to help you. If you are in a relationship with abuse, please know there are those who want to help you. My prayers are with you. My mother stayed in an abusive relationship for sixteen years before she had the courage to get help. It almost cost her life. Seek out the properly trained people and God will be a pleasant help to you.

Sometimes a lost job, marriage, family member, home, health problems, and the like can bring a feeling of defeat. Are you fighting feelings of defeat? Turn to someone who can help you sort out the truth from the lies. A counselor can help. Places to start are in the church, at a hospital, or reliable websites. For example, Focus on the Family is a great place to begin. Remember, to you and I the situation may appear to be defeated, but God views our situations differently. Trust and believe that He is in control. Let Him help.

"When we cannot see our way or cannot determine what to do, we do not need to be troubled at all concerning it, for the Lord Jehovah can see a way out of every complication".[25]

C. H. Spurgeon

---

25 C. H. Spurgeon (1997). Redeemed Souls Freed from Fear. Joy in Christ's presence (p. 106). New Kensington, PA: Whitaker House.

Chapter 6

The Place of Action

Are you a sports person? Perhaps NASCAR is your thing—the faster the better. Speed or watching things go fast winds you up. Maybe it's ice skating or *Who's Got Talent?* Watching how others perform effortlessly just boggles the mind. Maybe you are a runner and marathons are where your passion lies. Training accelerates you. Maybe teaching or being a firefighter gets you going, helping others to safety or to lift their hearts to a better life.

Whatever your passion, God says to do it for Him and to His glory no matter what He has called you to do (1 Corinthians 10:31). When God places us in a place of waiting, we can get pretty comfortable. And when God opens the door, moving may take a minute. Moving from waiting to serving can be like jumping off that bridge for the first time. We yell, "Give me a minute. I'm not ready."

Paul and Silas were passionate about sharing the gospel. When they landed in prison by way of releasing an imprisoned girl, they found themselves at a place of waiting. However, when God opened the door, they were ready to advance and used the opportunity to further the kingdom of God and presented the gospel to a whole family whose response was, "Yes, Lord." In their prison cell, Paul and Silas praised the Lord, waited for God's timing, and when the time came, they took advantage of the place they were in and stepped into the place of action.

We should never underestimate the place God has placed us, thinking God could never move beyond the current circumstances. It is a mistake to think that God only moves in churches or on the mission field. Of course He moves in these places. However, God can be seen by the witness you and I demonstrate in such places as the workplace, gym, school, and soccer field or at a NASCAR track. God is limitless, period.

Maybe you have been through many of the places this book describes, and now God says it's time to move. This can be as scary as waiting or as frightening as conflict or defeat. God has been using these places in your life to bring you to a place of usefulness, fruitfulness, and growth. Now the day is finally here. You have obeyed God and waited. You have learned, stretched, and maybe even rebelled, yet God has and will bring you through.

Paul and Silas in prison waited for God to release them, and through the jailer an opportunity presented itself. Paul and Silas boldly stepped out and into the guard's life and God moved, and by their obedience and action, salvation came. Paul and Silas persevered, and the ultimate question every believer waits to hear from those to whom they witnessed ran through the jail cell. The jailer asked Paul and Silas, "What must I do to be saved?" When the jailer realized that all the prisoners were accounted for, he responded as follows:

> And he called for lights and rushed in, and trembling with fear he fell down before Paul and Silas, and after he brought them out, he said, "Sirs, what must I do to be saved?" Paul and Silas responded. They said, "Believe in the Lord Jesus, and you will be saved, you and your household." And they spoke the word of the Lord to him together with all who were in his house. And he took them that very hour of the night and washed their wounds, and immediately he was baptized, he and all his household. And he brought them into his house and set food before them, and rejoiced greatly, having believed in God with his whole household. (Acts 16:29–34)

Every true believer wants to hear those words, "What must I do to be saved?" (See this website for the answer to this question: https://bible.org/article/gods-plan-salvation. You can also look in the back of the book.) We have prayed and waited for that loved one, friend, or coworker to ask that most-important question. After all they have been through ... man, what a moment. Paul and Silas wasted no time in sharing the gospel of Christ. How about you? Are you wondering what God has been doing and teaching you through all your trials? Has the time finally come to move? What is the first step? This is God territory, like all other areas of our lives, so be a prepared prayer warrior and make the most of every place where God has you. Paul and Silas had been praying in their cell (Acts 16:25) and were prayerfully ready when those doors swung open. After praying, praising, and seeking God, they were now ready for action. Let's *go*!

Try That Again!

What part of the battle as a Christian soldier are you called to fight? Are you a teacher? Wow, are you special. Teaching today is a challenge to say the least, with long hours, low pay, and the students. Bless their hearts, students today have many challenges, and the teacher has to help the total student overcome many of these challenges. But you, like Paul and Silas, keep marching forward. Giving up is not in your definition. Are you a firefighter or police office? Awesome. This job wears on you, does it not? Your job is to serve the community, and sometimes that community is hard and wears on your already tried state. Be encouraged. You are needed. How about the waitress? Is this you? Working with the public has its rewards and its frustrations. Long hours and little or no appreciation can lead us to the lack of action. Having been a waitress as a young woman, I appreciate those who serve us in restaurants. I understand and respect your job.

Whatever your position, there are challenges to meet daily. The guard who guarded Paul and Silas was doing his job. When those doors opened to the cell that night, he never dreamed his life would change forever. Are you a preacher, Sunday school teacher, or missionary? Paul and Silas simply wanted to share the gospel and encourage others, and look at their predicament. You know full well of the demands thrown your way daily. Are you a factory worker or a laborer? This is hard work, back breaking and difficult to say the least. Are you a stay-at-home mom? This is one of the most important positions you could hold.

What we do matters to God. He sees our efforts. He knows. Are you in a vocation that just wears you out day in and day out? Your boss does not get you. Your boss wants more and more and more, only to want more. Gratitude is not in your boss's vocabulary. However, you wait on the Lord and pray daily for His divine intervention.

I cannot pretend that I have the answer to your place; however, I do know when you serve God, He is faithful (Psalms 34:17, 37:23–24). Whether He calls us to stand and wait or stand and fight, He will give us the means to do so. Don't quit! Don't give in! Don't surrender! Don't let the Enemy trick you or convince you that if God has called you to do something that it won't work. You have waited, you have stood, and now God says it's time to move.

The tragic place is when we as Christians listen to the wrong voice. The Enemy says, "Wait a minute, you can't do that. How are you going to pay for that? How are you going to work that out? Are you kidding me? That will never work." Or perhaps he says, "How many times are you going to try that? Haven't you been humiliated enough, give it up" (just to mention a small few). This place of action is based on the prayer life you have demonstrated before God. Therefore if God has told you to move and you step out in faith, keep moving. Now suppose you step out in obedience and the first attempt seems to backfire or doesn't work. Do you quit? Of course not. Paul went to jail many times, but he never quit sharing the gospel. He wrote many letters from prison, yet he never quit ("Ephesians, Philippians, Colossians, and Philemon are called the 'prison' epistles because they were written by Paul during his imprisonment mentioned in Acts 28.")[26]

No matter what the outcome, keep moving forward. God has everything under control. "The Lord has established His throne in the heavens, and His sovereignty rules over all" (Psalm 103:19). Paul and Silas could have escaped that night from the prison cell. However, Paul realized God had a greater plan, and they remained. When what you do for the Lord appears to have holes in it, He is still in control, and remember our God can use anything and anybody to further His goal and purpose.

What do you do when it seems there are more brick walls than doors as you continue to move forward with the will of God? Remind yourself of this truth—when God moves you from one place to another, it doesn't mean the testing or trials are over. It means God is still working out His plan.

Paul and Silas saw a victorious sight when the jailer and his family came to salvation through Christ. Yet for them the battle was not over. Further inspection of the text shows Paul and Silas would face a different battle—the battle with the magistrates. In

---

26   B. Bright. (n.d.). Prison Epistles, Thessalonians, Pastoral Epistles. :: Cru. Retrieved June 2, 2014, from http://www.cru.org/training-and-growth/classics/10-basic-steps/10-the-new-testament/07-epistles.htm

Acts 16:20, 22, 35, 36, 38, the Greek term *strategos*, "magistrate," means captain, officer.[27] These were the go-to people when you had a dispute. Paul and Silas had been brought before them and accused of making trouble. The events unfolded, and a whole family found Christ. The day after these events, the magistrates sent word to set them free.

Now here is where some may struggle a bit. Paul said, "Now wait a minute, you have beaten, jailed, and accused us, and now you just want to set us free. You tell them to come themselves and face us."

> Now when day came, the chief magistrates sent their policemen, saying, "Release those men." And the jailer reported these words to Paul, saying, "The chief magistrates have sent to release you. Therefore come out now and go in peace." But Paul said to them, "They have beaten us in public without trial, men who are Romans, and have thrown us into prison; and now are they sending us away secretly? No indeed! But let them come themselves and bring us out. The policemen reported these words to the chief magistrates. They were afraid when they heard that they were Romans, and they came and appealed to them, and when they had brought them out, they kept begging them to leave the city.

---

27 E. W. Goodrick & J. R. Kohlenberger (2004). Greek to English dictionary and Index. The strongest NIV exhaustive concordance (p. 5074). Grand Rapids, Mich.: Zondervan.

> They went out of the prison and entered the house of Lydia, and when they saw the brethren, they encouraged them and departed. (Acts 16:35–40)

The struggle for some may be this: Why didn't Paul just come out, count his blessings, and go home? In the day of Paul, it was against the law for a Roman citizen to be treated in such a manner.[28] Paul stood his ground, and when he announced he was a Roman citizen, you can imagine the anxiety the magistrate felt. This new place Paul and Silas found themselves in called for standing their ground. Just because God moves us to a different location does not mean the battle is over. We have more ground to cover.

Paul was not through. He had gone from a place of waiting to a place of action. Has God now moved you to a place of action and you find yourself in doubt as to your calling? Are you questioning the voice of God and wonder if you heard clearly? Hang on. The place of action God has called you to have not changed. Road blocks, conflicts, and the like may very well be a part of God's plan.

The magistrates did come to release Paul and Silas but not with haughty spirits. This time there was fear and trembling. Like the place of waiting, this place of action may be as much for the benefit of another as it is for you and me. The place of action and confrontation, however, should always be at God's direction and not our own, bathed in prayer and readied by God's Word.

---

28   C. E. Arnold *Acts*. Grand Rapids, MI: Zondervan, 2007. (p.162).

When I attended school, an instructor asked me about my goals. My response was, "God has called me to teach and write." With the printing of this book, you may say, "Well, you did it." Yet an instructor in school did not believe God would lead a person like me to write. Let's face it, at the writing of this book, which is my first book, I am fifty-six. I manage a retail store. I am no scholar and neither am I on the bestsellers list, yet God has a purpose, and I am obedient. The way I see it, if one person reads these words and is encouraged or drawn to Christ, the gain is God's glory revealed. So have there been obstacles or road blocks? Of course. Did I ever once want to give it up? Of course, a number of times, yet I believed God and kept moving forward. With this said, what should we do in this place of action when God says move?

How it works!

1. *Trust and believe God.* Psalm 28:7 says, "The Lord is my strength and my shield; my heart *trusts in Him*, and I am helped; therefore my heart exults, and with my song I shall thank Him." Paul and Silas could have made a run for it; however, they waited and trusted God with the end results. The jailer, believing all was lost, sought to take things into his own hands and end it all, yet God intervened and the jailer believed God. Believing God seems so simple, yet it is more than just saying you believe God or in God. Our believing is acted out. Jesus said, "I am the way, and the truth, and the life; no one comes to the Father but through

Me."(John 14:6) It is not enough to believe in God; we must trust in Jesus. Take that step of faith and believe God to take care of you. This is the first step. Second, If God has called you to a particular place to serve, trust Him. First Thessalonians 5:24 says, "Faithful is He who calls you, and He also will bring it to pass." Continue in the direction He leads, and don't look back (unless it is to remind yourself of God's faithfulness).

2. *Keep serving.* Romans 12:10–13 says, "Be devoted to one another in brotherly love; give preference to one another in honor; not lagging behind in diligence, fervent in spirit, *serving the Lord*; rejoicing in hope, *persevering in tribulation*, devoted to prayer, contributing to the needs of the saints, practicing hospitality." Do not give up! Keep on moving till God closes the door, or in Paul and Silas's case, opens a door. When God moves you and trouble seems to follow, keep serving. Trust God. He knows what's going on. Remember, our God always has a plan.

3. *Be prepared to stand.* Ephesians 6:13 says, "Therefore, take up the full armor of God, so that you will be able to resist in the evil day, and having done everything, to stand firm." Paul and Silas were set free. However, Paul knew he had to make a stand. His plan of action was not to cause more trouble, but the plan was to stand his ground against the wrong accusations and wrongful treatment. Notice this was not about revenge or retaliation. This was Paul bringing to the attention of the authorities the wrong choices that were made (this could be another message altogether). Just

because God moves you does not mean the battle is over. Be prepared to stand. Be planted in the assurance God is in control, and just as He guides through places of conflict, defeat, waiting, and more, He will guide you in your place of action as well. When Stephen was martyred in Acts 7, where was Paul (or Saul, as he was known then)? In Acts 16, where was he? What a transformation. Saul went from being the accuser to the accused. However, now he stood in a different place and was willing to take action for the furtherance of God's kingdom and making a stand when needed. Are you and I ready to take such action and stand when needed?

4. *When it is time to take action, move!* Joshua 1:1–3 says, "Now it came about after the death of Moses the servant of the Lord, that the Lord spoke to Joshua the son of Nun, Moses' servant, saying, 'Moses My servant is dead; *now therefore arise*, cross this Jordan, you and all this people, to the land which I am giving to them, to the sons of Israel. Every place on which the sole of your foot treads, I have given it to you, just as I spoke to Moses.'" There will come a day when God says, "Arise, move, go," and it is vital for us to be prepared. The places we find ourselves in, like that of waiting, conflict, or defeat, prepare us for the move ahead. Read about the life of Joshua and see that he had grounds of preparations before he took over for Moses. In my own life, there has been much preparation for the place God has led me. He will do the same for you. Let our loving, caring heavenly Father prepare you, and when the time comes,

move. Read the Word, go to church, fellowship with other Christians, and share the gospel. Your time will come. It is time to move, pray, and follow Jesus as He leads.

"Prayer may seem at first like disengagement, a reflective time to consider God's point of view. But that vantage presses us back to accomplish God's will, the work of the kingdom. We are God's fellow workers, and as such we turn to prayer to equip us for the partnership".[29]

Philip Yancey

29 P. Yancey (2006). What Difference Does it Make?. Prayer: does it make any difference? (p. 128). Grand Rapids, Mich.: Zondervan.

Chapter 7

The Most of This Place: Focus

How well do you focus on details? My husband restores vintage motorcycles. He also from time to time shows these bikes. He has won a number of trophies for the bikes he restores. One reason for this is his eye for detail. He takes many months and pays close attention to the details of each and every bike he restores. They are details you and I may never see, but nevertheless he focuses on every little detail. The end result is a beautiful bike ready to show.

When we find ourselves in a particular place like that of waiting, defeat, conflict, or perhaps some other place, where we choose to place our focus makes a difference for how beautiful the outcome will be. The details of our actions, attitudes, mind-set, and motives determine our spiritual growth and perhaps the next step in our journey with Christ. How we respond is of the utmost importance. Pay attention to the details. Focus on what God has for you in the place where you now rest, and fight the urge to focus on the place. Place your attention on the one who designed your current place. Paul and Silas, when they were in prison, paid attention to the details. When those prison doors swung open, they did not rush out. They waited on the Lord, and He did not disappoint. The jailer was in need of a Savior, and Paul and Silas were in the right place at the appointed time and salvation came. Ask God for clear vision so you can witness the details.

Let's define focus. It is "the center of interest activity." Synonyms for focus are center, focal point, central point, center of attention, hub, nucleus, heart, core, and cornerstone.[30]

The focus of this book has been to relate the importance of making the most of every place God places you, no matter where it may be. We can learn no matter where God places us. You can tell a person's focus by what preoccupies his or her thoughts. During football season, this is the buzz. When working at a retail store during football season, the discussion often starts with, "Who is your team?" Then it progresses into why their team isn't winning, and from there it goes into whose quarterback is the most successful. The same goes for any sport or activity.

For example, at a family gathering the babies will get the focus hands down or perhaps the new graduate from high school. At

---

30 "Definition of Focus in English." Focus: definition of focus in Oxford dictionary (American English). N.p., n.d. Web. 10 Aug. 2014. http://www. oxforddictionaries.com/definition.

a wedding the bride shines. In church the pastor or perhaps the musician shines. It seems to reason that if we desire to make the most of the places God has placed us, our focus should be on the author of that place. When we choose to focus on Christ rather than on the place, we now can witness some amazing events. The place gets brighter. The place looks different. We begin to see clearly. Suddenly this place begins to take on purpose and meaning. Granted, this is a process, and things move according to God's timing. However when our focus moves to the one who opens and closes the door, our perspective begins to change, and this is where we see the hand of God.

Be Faithful Where You Are

When our focus is on Christ and following His will, things begin to change. We begin to desire what He desires, and we want to serve wholeheartedly. Paul and Silas had a focus, and that focus was to share the good news. When Paul and Silas ended up in prison, that focus stayed the same. By staying focused, Paul and Silas was able to lead the jailer and his family to the Savior. When God has seen fit to put you in a certain place at a certain time, understand God has a divine plan. Do not lose focus on His plan. Do not lose focus on His hand or His heart. Be faithful where God has you. Stay focused on His Word, and be devoted to prayer.

When I was in my early thirties, God revealed to me that He had a plan for my life. I was thrilled. I began to plan and follow His plan for my life. Now I must say I expected His plan to unfold in about six months. You know God said it, and it is surely done.

This I believe. However, His time clock is not in line with mine. So I have waited and waited, and still I wait. There have been a couple of times when I have almost abandoned this call. With no doors to open, I figured I heard wrong and I would just give up this notion He gave to me. Yet something inside me will not let me give up. I keep moving ahead, trusting He spoke to my heart and in His time the right door will open.

One thing God has made abundantly clear is that while He may not have me where I believe He will one day, He has me in another place where I must serve Him just as faithfully. So as I wait I serve with all my heart. And when this place gets unbearable—and it does—I make sure I keep my focus on my Creator and Savior and the door keeper. I give all my best to His glory—not my leftover from yesterday, my best for today and my first fruits of all my service to Him.

Believe God Wants the Best for You

When Paul and Silas were released from prison, they went to Lydia's house to share all they had witnessed. Acts 16:40 says, "They went out of the prison and entered the house of Lydia, and when they saw the brethren, they encouraged them and departed." Even though Paul and Silas had been through quite a place, their focus stayed on the purpose of their calling. They were encouraged by all the events because God had used and delivered them. They knew the Lord was with them and He cared about every area they had been through.

God demonstrated His love for the jailer and His family, and He demonstrates His love for you and me by reminding us that He has a plan for our life. This should be our focus as we walk with Christ. Never lose sight of the fact He loves us and He has a plan for each of us. Jeremiah 29:11 says, "'For I know the plans that I have for you,' declares the Lord, 'plans for welfare and not for calamity to give you a future and a hope.'" Understand that in the place you stand right now, wherever or whatever it may be, resides a beautiful Savior to help you through.

Some Promises to Focus on

> For as many as are the promises of God, in Him they are yes; therefore also through Him is our Amen to the glory of God through us. (2 Corinthians 1:20)

1. Joshua 21:45 says, "Not one of the good promises which the Lord had made to the house of Israel failed; all came to pass." (God promises are always true.)

2. John 16:23 says, "In that day you will not question Me about anything. Truly, truly, I say to you, if you ask the Father for anything in My name, He will give it to you." (No matter where your place may be, you can call to Him. He hears and will come.)

3. Hebrews 11:13 says, "All these died in faith, without receiving the promises, but having seen them and having welcomed them from a distance, and having confessed that they were strangers and exiles on the earth." (Trust what

God has promised and said no matter what. Believe He loves you and knows your situation. Trust Him and stay focused on Him even if you cannot see the future.)

4. Second Peter 1:4 says, "For by these He has granted to us His precious and magnificent promises, so that by them you may become partakers of the divine nature, having escaped the corruption that is in the world by lust." (God desires for you and me to grow. The place He has you is part of that growth. Let Him do His work. Trust Him and know and find comfort in this truth.)

5. Hebrews 13:5 says, "Make sure that your character is free from the love of money, being content with what you have; *for He Himself has said, "I will never desert you, nor will I ever forsake you." (God is in the middle with you and plans to stay there.)*

6. Isaiah 26:3 says, "The steadfast of mind You will keep in perfect peace, Because he trusts in You." (God wants to give you peace in the place He has you. Trust Him to do just that.)

Conclusion

This study has been set forth to bring us to a place of surrender where God has us. No matter where your place may be, you can find purpose and hope. I remember standing beside the bed of my dear mom as the Lord was preparing to take her home. Like many of you, I had mixed emotions. I did not want my mom to suffer. However, I desired her in my life. What purpose could this possibly have? Questions flooded my soul. Why now? Why her? What was I to do? I will never forget as my mom took her last breath, we began to sing "Amazing Grace." A peace came to me I will never forget and look to even now some years later. God kept His promise, and peace was mine. Whatever the place God has you, remember He loves you like no other. He sacrificed like no other. And His plan is like no other plan. To make the most of this place takes courage, strength, and a Christ-centered focus. Watch and see the treasures you will take with you as you make the most of this place.

God's Plan for Salvation

We are all sinners. "For all have sinned and come short of the glory of God" (Romans 3:23). Sin is anything that is not pleasing to God. One sin keeps us from heaven; therefore none can go to heaven. We all come short, and our fellowship with God is broken. We are lost, on our own, and doomed for hell. "For the wages of sin is death, but the gift of God is eternal life through Jesus Christ our Lord" (Romans 6:23). God, however, had a plan. He would send His only perfect Son for the salvation of the world. "For God so loved the world that He gave His only Son, that whosoever believes in Him should not perish but have everlasting life" (John 3:16). Through faith, by believing that Jesus died, was buried, and rose on the third day for our sins, we receive eternal life. "For by grace you have been saved through faith; and that not of yourselves, it is the gift of God; not as a result of works, so that no one may boast" (Ephesians 2:8–9).

No other way can bring salvation but through God's only Son, Jesus. "Jesus said to him, 'I am the way, and the truth, and the life; no one comes to the Father but through Me'" (John 14:6). When we pray and ask Jesus to forgive our sins and to come into our life and save us, He will. "Behold, I stand at the door and knock; if anyone hears My voice and opens the door, I will come in to him and will dine with him, and he with Me" (Revelation 3:20). The prayer of salvation goes something like this: "Jesus, I know I am a sinner. I have sinned against You. Please forgive me of my sins. Come into my life and save me and be my Lord and Savior. Thank You, Lord, for saving me." We accept Jesus by faith, and if you prayed this prayer, to God be the glory. I rejoice over you and your victory. The next thing to do is tell someone. Then find a Bible-believing church where you can grow with God's people. Let me know about your decision so I can pray for you and rejoice over you.

Bibliography

Arnold, C. E., *Acts*. Grand Rapids, MI: Zondervan, 2007. (p.162).

Baseball Plays: Sacrifice Play. (n.d.). Baseball Tutorials RSS. Retrieved March 3, 2014, from http://www.baseball-tutorials. com/baseball-plays-sacrifice-play/47/

Bright, B. (n.d.). Prison Epistles, Thessalonians, Pastoral Epistles. :: Cru. Retrieved June 2, 2014, from http://www.cru.org/training-and-growth/classics/10-basic-steps/10-the-new- testament/07-epistles.htm

Bruce, F. F., *The Book of the Acts* (Rev. ed.). Grand Rapids, MI: William B. Eerdmans Publishing Co., 1988. (p.317).

Bullock, C. (2001). Encountering the book of Psalms: A literary and theological introduction (p. 72). Grand Rapids, Mich.: Baker Academic.

Carson, D. A. (2010). Scandalous: the cross and resurrection of Jesus. Wheaton, Ill.: Crossway. E-book.

Christian Life and Witness Course (Rev. Ed.). Minneapolis, MN: Billy Graham Evangelistic Association, 1999.

Definition of blended family in English. (n.d.). Blended family: definition of blended family in Oxford dictionary (British & World English). Retrieved April 6, 2014, from http://www. oxforddictionaries.com/definition/english/blended-family

Definition of conflict in English: (n.d.). Conflict: definition of conflict in Oxford dictionary (American English) (US). Retrieved March 23, 2014, from http://www.oxforddictionaries.com/us/ definition/american_english/conflict

Definition of contentment in English:. (n.d.). Contentment: definition of contentment in Oxford dictionary (British & World English). Retrieved August 10, 2014, from http://www. oxforddictionaries.com/definition

Definition of defeat in English. Defeat: definition of defeat in Oxford dictionary (British & World English). N.P., n.d. Web. 10 Aug. 2014. http://www.oxforddictionaries.com/definition

Definition of focus in English. Focus: definition of focus in Oxford dictionary (American English). N.p., n.d. Web. 10 Aug. 2014. http://www.oxforddictionaries.com/definition

Definition of pain in English. (n.d.). Pain: definition of pain in Oxford dictionary (American English) (US). Retrieved March 3, 2014, from http://www.oxforddictionaries.com/us/definition/american_english/pain

Definition of self in English. (n.d.). Self: definition of self in Oxford dictionary (British & World English). Retrieved August 10, 2014, from http://www.oxforddictionaries.com/definition/english/self

Definition of wait in English. (n.d.). Wait: definition of wait in Oxford dictionary (British & World English). Retrieved August 10, 2014, from http://www.oxforddictionaries.com/definition

Earley, D., & Wheeler, D. A. (2010). Evangelism is: Not Following the Example of the Disciples. Evangelism is--: how to share Jesus with passion and confidence (p. 131). Nashville, Tenn.: B & H Academic.

Elliot, E. (1995). Waiting. Keep a quiet heart (p. 135). Ann Arbor, Mich.: Vine Books.

Erickson, M. J., *Christian Theology* (2nd ed.). Grand Rapids, MI: Baker Book House, 1998. (p.131)

Goodrick, E. W., & Kohlenberger, J. R. (2004). Greek to English dictionary and Index. The strongest NIV exhaustive concordance (p. 5074). Grand Rapids, Mich.: Zondervan.

Grow Your Faith. (n.d.). Billy Graham Evangelistic Association. Retrieved March 23, 2014, from http://billygraham.org/grow-your-faith/

History of the Chinese Finger Trap. (n.d.). Chinese Finger Traps Online, Chinese Finger Puzzle Handcuffs. Retrieved October 20, 2014, from http://www.chinesefingertrap.co.uk/page_4.ht

Jeremiah, D. (1994). The Write Way to Encourage. Acts of love: the power of encouragement (p. 152). Gresham, OR: Vision House.

Morgan, R. J. (2001). Waiting. The Red Sea rules: 10 God-given strategies for difficult times (p. 51). Nashville: T. Nelson.

Polhill, J. B., *Acts.* Nashville, TN: Broadman Press, 1992. (P. 352-353).

Spalding, E., Garcia, J., & Braun, J. A. *An Introduction to Standards-Based Reflective Practice for Middle and High School Teaching.* New York: Teachers College Press, 2010.

Spurgeon, C. H. (1997). Redeemed Souls Freed from Fear. Joy in Christ's presence (p. 106). New Kensington, PA: Whitaker House.

The Way of the Master. (n.d.). The Way of the Master. Retrieved March 23, 2014, from http://www.wayofthemaster.com/index.shtm

Welcome | Random Acts of Kindness. (n.d.). Welcome | Random Acts of Kindness. Retrieved April 12, 2014, from http://www.randomactsofkindness.org/

Wright, N. T. *Acts for Everyone*. Louisville, KY: Westminster John Knox Press, 2008, E-book.

Yancey, P. (2006). What Difference Does it Make?. Prayer: does it make any difference? (p. 128). Grand Rapids, Mich.: Zondervan.

Acknowledgments

To my Lord and Savior for His saving grace. To God is the glory.
To my husband for your precious perseverance.
To the publisher of this book …
my humble thank you!

Printed in the United States
By Bookmasters